FAITH, LOVE AND LIFE

*To: my FRIEND
Walter Wilson
Stanly E Alston*

# FAITH, LOVE AND LIFE

A Collection of Poems and Songs

By:
**Stanley E. Alston**

Magnatic Music
P.O. Box 2054
Woodbridge, Virginia 22195-2054

# Faith, Love and Life

Copyright © 2002 by Stanley E. Alston
Designs and Illustrations by: Sheila Y. Alston,
Proofread by: Angelique Sharps and
Isaiah E. Alston

All rights reserved. No part of this publication may be reproduced, stored in or introduced into a retrieval system, or transmitted, in any form, or by any means (electronic, mechanical, photocopying, recording or otherwise), without the prior written permission of the publisher.

First Edition

Ordering information:

Old School Entertainment by Stanley E. Alston
P.O. Box 2054
Woodbridge, VA 22195-2054
alstonsongs@aol.com

Library of Congress
**ISBN: 0-9719897-0-2**

## Contents

Inspirational ................................................ 6
Dedication .................................................. 7
Introduction ................................................ 8

**FAITH**
Jericho Road ............................................... 10
The Voice .................................................. 11
Within My Heart ........................................... 12
Wisdom Is .................................................. 13
Spirit Run Free ............................................ 14
No Such Thing As Can't .................................. 15
Someone's Watching ...................................... 16
Sky To Be Free ............................................ 17
How Far Away Is Heaven? ................................ 18
What Are Your Thoughts? ................................ 19
Do You Know About Jesus? .............................. 20
My Life Belongs To Jesus ................................ 22
Positive .................................................... 23
Separation ................................................. 24
Forgiveness ................................................ 25
Creation ................................................... 26
The Willow Chase Me ..................................... 27
Don't Weep For Me ....................................... 28
Leave It In God's Hand ................................... 29
I'm Gonna Tell Jesus ..................................... 30
A Cry For Help ............................................ 31
Thank GOD Enough ...................................... 32

## LOVE

| | |
|---|---|
| Love............................................................... | 34 |
| You're Beautiful, You're Special.................. | 35 |
| When Can I Love You?................................ | 36 |
| Chocolate Girl............................................. | 37 |
| Can't Stop Loving You................................ | 38 |
| Pillow of Love............................................. | 39 |
| I Care.......................................................... | 40 |
| I Love You................................................... | 41 |
| A Rose From The Garden........................... | 42 |
| Will You Stick By My Side?......................... | 43 |
| I'll Never Love Another............................... | 44 |
| Vintage Is Our Love.................................... | 45 |
| Someone I Used To Love............................ | 46 |
| After Love................................................... | 47 |
| When I'm Missing You................................ | 48 |
| Madness In Love........................................ | 49 |
| Be For Real................................................ | 50 |
| I Wish You Well........................................... | 51 |
| It's Deep Love............................................ | 52 |
| If I Had A Chance....................................... | 53 |
| Our Love Is Through................................... | 54 |
| Distance Love............................................. | 55 |
| What Would It Mean?.................................. | 56 |

## LIFE

| | |
|---|---|
| The Challenge............................................ | 58 |
| Why Worry.................................................. | 59 |
| Mom and Dad............................................. | 60 |
| I'd Rather Be Buried Dead! Than Alive!........ | 61 |
| Feel The Need To Be.................................. | 62 |
| Lessons Learned........................................ | 63 |
| Get The Monkey Off My Shoulder............... | 64 |
| Animal Attractions....................................... | 65 |
| Dance Town U.S.A...................................... | 66 |

Dream Your Dream.................................. 67
Anything You Want To Do........................ 68
Rise............................................................ 69
City Made Of Fire..................................... 70
Come To Me.............................................. 71
Is It True?................................................. 72
The Loneliest Man.................................... 73
It's Not Over Until It's Over..................... 74
Reach Out America................................... 75
Nine Eleven.............................................. 76
A Bird's Point of View.............................. 77
I Am a Poet............................................... 78
Bones and Biscuits................................... 79
Tonight We Are Going To Party................ 80
Wilson's.................................................... 81
Ghetto Child............................................. 82
So Far From Here..................................... 83
Teacher's Sight......................................... 84
The Street................................................. 87
Fade, Skin, Last Blade............................. 88
Conditioned.............................................. 89
Evelyn's Asleep........................................ 91
Duck The Axe........................................... 93
Yes, I Believe............................................ 94

*Special Thanks*........................................ 96

**2002 International Poet of Merit Award**
*Love*.......................................................... 34
**1986 Golden Poet Award**
*Chocolate Girl*......................................... 37
**Theme Song written for WJZ-TV, Baltimore, MD**
*Be for Real*.............................................. 50

## Inspirational

My inspirational and emotional creativity has been enlightened by human laughter and tears on this emotional roller coaster we call Life.

## Dedication

If I lived a million years, I could not thank GOD enough. For His creations are my inspirations.
I dedicate this work to my Wife, Mom, Dad, Sisters, Brothers, Neighbors and Friends.

## INTRODUCTION

Every ray of light gleams meaning to human life. Life is the essence of joy. I confess my love of humanity and pray to place words of substance in craving hearts. Our thoughts of passion, pain, and pleasure defined our faith.

*FAITH—*
*An absolute trust in GOD that the impossible can be accomplished.*

## JERICHO ROAD

Many paths I've journeyed
To life's purpose in time,
To find it's not easy—
The search for peace of mind.
The sunrise does guide me,
As deceit tries to blind me
In my travels down Jericho Road.

So many people, I'll meet along the way;
Some are hungry
While others just pray.
They all have tried;
Some have even died
In the journey down Jericho Road.

So I bid my friends good-bye.
Purpose beckons me to try.
Though the world seems cold,
It's a place where the young grow old.
For life can tease you,
As the stars guide you
In your journey down Jericho Road.

I wish I had a star
For every newborn babe to ride
Through the shadows.
Storms they are sure to find;
It's a chance we all must take.
Life's not a twist or shake.
You give and take down Jericho Road.

## THE VOICE

You hear me in your darkest nights,
Your morning light,
Your daytime flight.

I touch you with a smile unseen,
Reveal to you my inner dreams.
You call me in your needful hour
For I'm the Voice,
The Voice of power.

I'll bring you news
Of the day gone by.
I speak of rain, sunshine,
And clouds in the sky.

I'll tell you how to dress,
Where to go,
If it's fast or if it's slow,
What is right or what is wrong,
Provide you music,
Or just hum along.
You know me as the Voice unseen.

The special one
Deep in your dreams,
Tomorrow we'll start over again.
I'll be the choice, your Voice unseen.

## WITHIN MY HEART

When the Creator of all things made man,
He gifted him with the sufficient to survive
a beautiful planet full of life, with free,
winding streams.
Flowing through land as fertile as woman
Precious air sweeter, than the taste of honey,
Some men have sought to shortcut
The Creator's natural way of thinking.
They have forced oppression,
upon their fellow man.

For their own selfish gains,
Rather than for the gains and
Preservation of mankind.
Within my heart,
I feel that I was born
To reach out and enhance my fellow man
With the voice of a sword,
The spirit of forever,
And a heart of truth.

With the help of the Creator,
I'm positive I will reach my goals
And serve His purpose.

## WISDOM IS

Wisdom is knowing yourself
With humbleness.
This knowledge gives freedom of
self-motivation to deal with the obstacles
That may attempt to blind you.

The truth can't be hidden when there is light.
People shine to complete creations destiny.
Keep your life naturally vibrating,
Loving the life that's about you.

For there are gifts sent from above to comfort
you, so that your dreams come true.
Nothing can shake or break your heart.
And justice will come
By the life that you live
In harmony, peace, love,
Everyday we should give.
For peace is with the one
Who knows himself.

## SPIRITS RUN FREE

Last night I had a dream
About you and me.
Imagine you were warmly
Lying in my arms.
If I hadn't awakened
The world would be shaken,
But not you or I
'Cause Spirits Run Free.

Like birds chirp as words I speak.
Spirits Run Free just like you and me,
Just like you, surely like me.

I saw your face,
Bright as the night,
As it eclipse to be light,
It was so nice, but was it right!
To be a Spirit,
a Spirit in the night.

I must confess
I'd like to spend precious moments with you.
And it must be true
That you feel this way too,
'Cause Spirits Run Free.

I dream about you,
Yeah, you dream about me too.
Because Spirits run,
Yes, Spirits Run Free.

## NO SUCH THING AS CAN'T

Never understood anything my Dad would say
He told me all things were possible,
If you would just believe.
He was not an overly religious man.
I think it's because he lost both parents
at a very young age.

Dad didn't have much book education,
But in my eyes wasn't much my Dad couldn't
do he'd say things like the Jack-of-all-trades
And the master of none.

Only a few things did Dad really believe --
Work real hard trusts in God,
And love our nation.

Sometimes, when he was in a spirited mood,
He went a yelling,
"Never want what you can't afford.
Don't borrow what you can't repay.
Don't break, what you can't fix.
And don't loan what you can't afford to lose."

Another strange thing he'd say was,
"If it's of the flesh you can't judge me,
Because of skin you don't see me."
So as I strive to find my spirituality,
I remember what my Dad taught me.
there's No Such Thing As Can't.

## SOMEONE'S WATCHING

Hold fast to the faith
That you have,
For the cloud that's upon you will pass.
The sun will smile upon your head.
Someone's Watching, waiting to see
What my brothers are going to do today.
With all the distrust,
Heart-warming lust,
Could this someone
Be you or me?

Now, I'm not to judge you
Nor you to judge me,
For our hearts are crying
And they want to be free.
Now it's been written and said that
The meek shall inherit the earth.
For they have thirst and the day is
Coming to be first.
Someone's Watching, can't you see?

## SKY TO BE FREE

People work from day to day
With displeasure in their hearts,
Seeking to find a little peace of mind
That makes them all apart
They are never in the rhythmic
Patterns of their lives.
So search the sky to be free;
It's above the earth to see.
And gather hope from despair;
it's comfort to know one cares.
There are no purposes in life except the one
For which you were born.
So no matter what ever,
It's hope that you gather.
In the effort to find your way
Reaching a scale of ten
Not knowing where to begin.
Sky to be free.

Search the sky to be free;
It's above the earth to see.
And gather hope from despair;
it's comfort to know one cares.

## HOW FAR AWAY IS HEAVEN?

How far away is heaven?
Nearer than what we think.
Alive with birds and bees
Could heaven be the sun
That shines in my eyes
With the morning light?
Or could it be the rain that sings
To the delight of a farmer's needs?
Oh yes, yes, yes, indeed.

Heaven to me is all that I see—
All that is real to life minus my fantasy.
Heaven is the meow of a kitten
And the bow-wow of a dog.

It's the roar of the sea,
Crashing against its shores
Endlessly day after day,
And night after night,
With the power and beauty of time;
Hour after hour after hour!

## WHAT ARE YOUR THOUGHTS?

What do you think of—
The flowers that grow about you,
The sun that beams through,
the eyes of the wind?
Do you wish upon a star,
Or just walk in the park
With the one you love?

Do you watch the rainfall with delight—
Singling out each drop in flight;
Or just daydream,
And wonder who created it all?
Are you at a loss for the time
And place to express yourself;
Your joys, your sorrows?
Or are you just grateful to be alive?

Do you admire how the birds fly high,
And the fish swim, and the wind blows on
through time and space?
Would you rather be a king
Who sits on a throne
Or a Casanova who loves to roam?

Would you have so much money
Until it's funny, and laugh without a friend?
Do you question day and night,
Wrong, or right?
Who creates the sound and light—
Have the will and the might?
What do you think of?

## DO YOU KNOW ABOUT JESUS?

When you're caught in a battle that you know
you can't win.
No one to turn to, nowhere to begin,
You need 2 know about Jesus the # 1 soldier;
You need 2 know about Jesus He's my savior.

When you're in trouble in need of a friend,
Someone to listen on whom you can depend,
Do You Know About Jesus? You need to know
about Jesus.
If you're lost, He can find you in the darkness
of the night.
If you are hungry, He will feed you with the
bread known as life.
If there's a battle that you're losing from the
fierceness of the fight,

You need 2 know about Jesus, the # 1 soldier;
You need 2 know about Jesus, He's my savior.
Do You Know About Jesus? You need to know
about Jesus.
(Repeat—Refrain)

If you're lost, He can find you in the darkness
of the night.
If you are ill, the Lord can heal you with the
goodness of his might.

FAITH, LOVE AND LIFE

If you are hungry, He will feed you with the bread known as life.
If there's a battle that you're losing from the fierceness of the fight,

You need 2 know about Jesus, the # 1 soldier.
You need 2 know about Jesus, He's my savior.
(Repeat—Refrain)

## MY LIFE BELONGS TO JESUS

My life belongs to Jesus.
My life belongs to Jesus.
My life belongs to Jesus,
Because He cared for me in time of need!

Not long ago my life was filled with gloom,
Found that my roses were bittersweet.
Turned to the only true God I knew!
And He came to my rescue!

That's why
My life, my life belongs to Jesus.
My life, my life belongs to Jesus.
My life, my life belongs to Jesus,
Because He cared for me in time of need.

He gives me breath, when I'm lost for life,
Restores my dreams when I cannot sleep.
He heals this old lonely heart and soul of mine.
And He can do the same for you.
That's why
My life belongs to Jesus; my life belongs to Jesus.

No longer do I wonder if I'm right or wrong.
You see my God, my God can make the weakest stand strong.
He heals this old lonely heart and soul of mine.
That's why
My heart, my Life, my soul belongs to Him.

## *POSITIVE—*

Though my oppressors would seek to
Drain my hidden strengths,
I must not allow my positive conscious
State of being disrupted.
My divine and merciful Creator guides
And protects my every step.

## *SEPARATION—*

Let not the parting of our physical beings
Lead to the separation of our Hearts.

## *FORGIVENESS—*

May our hearts be gifted with
forgiveness of our mistakes.
Let your heart be as a clear cool stream pure
with the taste of thought, rich with the
minerals of eternity, Free of fear to love.

## *CREATION—*

God's gift to man is creation. The gift of creation
is understanding. Through understanding we
learn to appreciate the gift of life and to know
ourselves. Have you ever thought about
the things that mean the most to you,
And begin to cry? That's love.

## THE WILLOW CHASED ME

It started one summer morning
As the birds gazed in jealousy.
It continued that afternoon beneath
The scorching sun.
I wanted to stop under a shaded tree
In the bushy forest,
But The Willow Chased Me.
Up a steep hill,
Through a narrow path,
Down a small road,
Across a shallow stream,
The Willow Chased Me.
As night began to fall,
The owls watched
And began to kook.
Small animals ran by
As other moved carefully.
I ran all night, until my breath
Became the morning dew—
As the willow chased no more,
It's now chasing you.

## DON'T WEEP FOR ME

I've lived my life to the fullness of my being,
Had a few good times, laughed a minute,
Enjoyed a good meal or two.
But when my light glows no more,
Don't Weep For Me, don't you dare weep for me.

If I could rise up and live my life over again,
The only thing I would try to change is a wish
that I could bring more sunshine into your life.
Don't Weep For Me, don't you dare weep for me.

And when they play the music,
Let it be the music of my life;
may it be the joy of joys.
Let it be the sound of happiness.
Don't weep, don't weep, Don't Weep For Me.

I have heard the birds sing, and the laughter
children bring.
My life was not in vain;
So don't you dare, because I care,
Don't Weep For Me.

## LEAVE IT IN GOD'S HAND

Some people worry about whether tomorrow will ever come.
Some folks worry to be worrying; others may call it dumb.
I can't answer for you, nor tell you your dreams will come true.

For I'm no saint, and have no crystal ball.
But one word of advice I'd give to you.
If you don't understand what's happening in this world,
Don't turn your back on your faith.
Pray harder and harder everyday.

Don't worry about where you're going to lay your head;
Nor about Monday or what people may say.
They're searching to find their way;
Leave It In God's Hands.

## I'M GONNA TELL JESUS

Lord, my heavenly Father
I want to speak with you,
Speak to my GOD.
I've got so much I want to share
From the bottom of my heart
Heavenly Father, all eyes are upon you.
There are a lot of unhappy people.
You're our Redeemer,
The answer to our every prayer.

Lord do you still hear us?
Will you come and answer our prayers?
Many can't handle it.
Children are crying;
Old folks, they are dying.
Where are you, Jesus?
Are you too deep within our hearts?

## A CRY FOR HELP

Lord knows I've tried
With all the strength given,
To do what You have me to do.
But the road keeps getting narrow
And the load grows with each passing day.

Help me, please, Father.
Show me the way.
I've come too far, I'm never going to stray.
Lost some worldly possessions,
Friends, that were, never to be.
But I'll never turn my back on You.
I'm going to keep reaching
And climbing everyday.
Most of all,
I'll keep believing in you.

## THANK GOD ENOUGH

If I lived a million years,
I could not Thank God Enough.
Some live for jobs, cars, or fancy things that
Life might bring.
I humble myself before You, God and give grace
For everything,
Knowing I could never repay Your? love.
From the highest mountain
Or the bluest sea,
I could not Thank God Enough.
The birds tweet sweet melodies to wake me
As the sun lights the horizon.
Stars blanket my body as I rest in Your arms.
I could not Thank God Enough

For the kind words upon this earth
That nourishes my soul
Every second, minute, moment I breathe,
I could not Thank God Enough.
I've seen mountains, beauty to adore
Taste water, felt the sun in my face
Walked in the rain, played in the snow.
I've rolled down hills, danced across lily fields.
I would not know where to begin to thank God.
I could not Thank God Enough!

## *LOVE* –

*The ability to forgive, rebuild, and Appreciate the Essence of living.*

## LOVE

One day these eyes are going to close.
Like the window of the eye,
behind the clouds of a shattered door.
And I won't say what I missed or whom I
kissed, who I loved, or failed to embrace.
When that day comes, I'll walk no more,
like once before as you and I knew but as a
memory— remembering me as the stars, the
wind, the mountainous trees or cool
summer breeze.
Rather, you and me, a touch, a smile
or softly spoken word that said little—
But meant so much.
O yes, one day these eyes shall close?
No, will close as the dust to a pebble rose,
to reveal what has been concealed
until now through the stillness
of his will. And I shall pass just as time—
beyond infinite moments in the space of
your mind. And you will realize how much you
loved me as I realize how much I loved you.

## YOU'RE BEAUTIFUL, YOU'RE SPECIAL

You're truly special to a world
That's in need of so much love.
Warm passion and desire
To take life higher, on the plain
For which we should be.
You're truly everything
That matters to me.
You're the sun and the moon,
The night and the day.
You're a cool breeze
to quench my thirst
on a hot summer's night.
I like your eyes
They're brown as mine,
green as the grass,
blue as the sky.
The sun and the moon—
You're special
to a world that's in need
of so much love—
So very, very special.
And you're beautiful to me.

## WHEN CAN I LOVE YOU?

The clock is quickly,
Quickly turning on the wall.
Catch my love, baby,
Before you lose it all.
I'm yours for now,
But tomorrow may never come.
So answer, lady,
Please don't make me wait too long!
When if? When Can I Love You? I need to know
When baby, if baby, When Can I Love You?

Don't make a promise to me, lady,
One that you cannot keep.
So much love, so much rhythm
Deep within your eyes I see.
And patiently I've waited
To whisper sweet harmonies.
It's getting harder by the hour to resist your company.
When If? When Can I Love You? I need to know
When baby, if baby, When Can I Love You?
I'm out of control, I've got to know, I need to know
When baby if? When Can I Love You? I need to know
When baby, if baby, When Can I Love You?

## CHOCOLATE GIRL

A mystery you are to me,
With beauty that opens my eyes to see
Skin smooth as velvet fire.
Eyes like stars that lift me higher
As no other in this world to compare,
Warmth of the sun in crisp winter's air
Cool as the breeze,
Shade to a burning part,
Loving you with all my heart.
So tender you are
With each and every
Word that you say.
Building trust on love's foundation day to day,
And it's no wonder that others
Would admire your style and grace.
For lady, you are sensitive to others.
You control and set the pace.
I have no fear in ever losing you.
Though many would try to share a joy or two,
Instead I'll cherish the moments
When you're by my side,
Strong dark and chocolate—
Taking life in stride.

### CAN'T STOP LOVING YOU

I can do anything that any other man can do—
Dance, make romance till the crack of dawn.
But I can't, no I can't, for the life of me
Forget the joy we once shared in love.
But I can't, no I can't, stop loving you.

Your memories always come shining through.
People ask me why I love to party down,
To dance the memory of your love away.

People ask me why I sometimes sit and stare
And I guess it's because, I still really care.
But I can't, no I can't stop loving you.
Your memories always come shining through.

FAITH, LOVE AND LIFE

## PILLOW OF LOVE

Many men have tried
To be the joy in your eyes,
Be that special delight and sleep with you
through the night.
What they don't know is that
I'm with you in the night—
Forever with you, squeeze me baby, ooh just right.
I'm your pillow baby, with you every night.
I'm your pillow baby, your
Pillow of Love.
When you're unhappy from what the
day has put you through,
You rest your head on my shoulder and I whisper
sweet? tender words to you.
For I know just what you're going through.
'Cause I'm your pillow baby, your
Pillow of Love.

In the middle of the night,
When everyone is sound asleep,
We play games of love; we kiss and hug.
Sometimes we even rub.
From dust to dawn you're always in my arms.
'Cause I'm your pillow baby, with you every night.
I'm your pillow baby, your
Pillow of Love.
I hear your prayers; we pray for the same things too.
To be together, forever my love.
Through stormy weather, I'll be by your side.
'Cause I'm your pillow baby, your
Pillow of Love!

## I CARE

I watch you as you open your eyes
To the first sight of life, little girl.
And I wonder how it feels, or is life really real.
Your body seems so thin and small,
But you will grow tall, my dear.
And how wonderful your heart must be,
For it's free and knows no fear.
But no matter how strange
It all must seem to you,
Daddy's here and he cares.
The laws of life I must teach you
For they are not really fair.
So let me tell you my first-born child,
All thought the sun may shine so bright
In your crystal clear eyes.
I must explain the rain and the game
That is sometimes played.
Not because games are there
Nor in love games are fair,
But because I care!

## I LOVE YOU

It's hard to imagine that anyone could love me
As much as you do, baby.
After all the things I've done, that your love
Could grow even more so true.
I've thought for many days of all the kind,
Ways to say that I really love you too.
Yes, I do.

But as you know, I've been hurt so many times.
And my feelings are hidden so deep inside.
Will you forgive me if I stumble?
It's not because I wonder.
Will you forgive me if I don't say goodnight?
It's not because we've had a fight.
I really love you.
Yes, I do.

And when we step out in the light,
Remember all eyes; we're in sight.
And when the man says do you
Remember I love you too,
It's not hard to remember
Because it's so true.
I really love you.
Yes, I do.

## A ROSE FROM THE GARDEN

You smell sweet—
Beauty that's divine.
Many sought to imitate
This gift protected by it own beauty—
None to duplicate
Or deny its selfish thorns.
Many desire to hold and control
Bee buzz with envy.
Plants mingle about you.
They relish you in home fields,
Houses built especially to embrace you.
I adore your mystery of pain and pleasure.
The wind dances to your sight and smell.
I'd like to dance alone with you,
But you bring life and joy to many.
The sun caresses you each day
As the rain plays a game that becomes you.
You are ordained by sights unseen—
Earth's prized possession.
I'm happy to gaze upon you,
And smell your sweet nectar.
You are A Rose From the Garden.

## WILL YOU STICK BY MY SIDE?

When the lights are turned down low
And the curtain begins to close,
who'll be by your side?
When the nights are also cold,
Will you hear the whispers, with stories untold?
And if by chance you should see my dreams
Melt before your eyes; tell me, dear lady,
would you stick by my side?

If the moon would suddenly disappear,
And lovers' hearts reacted in fear,
Have faith in me.
And if the sun would suddenly cease to shine,
And faces were impossible to find,
Hear my heart beat—
And if by chance you should see my dreams
Melt before you eyes; tell me, dear lady,
would you stick by my side?

I've said all the things that words can express,
But nothing like a heart
says it the best— the tenderness of love.
The stars that shine in the night have
no meaning without your love.
And if by chance you should see my dreams
Melt before you eyes; tell me, dear lady,
would you stick by my side?

## I'LL NEVER LOVE ANOTHER

I will never love anyone, like you girl.
I will never love another—
For you, its' been so long—
Since I have held you in my arms, girl
And filled you with my love charms.
From your toes to the tip of your nose
I would like to love you through all eternity.

When you laugh, your smile just fills my heart
With a feeling words were not meant to express.
So stay with me and never leave.
For I have never met anyone like you.

Many people admire your tenderness,
And your honesty could bring a heart to shame.
I will play no games to express my love
For without you, I could not go on.

## VINTAGE IS OUR LOVE

A man walks a lonely path
Sometimes paved with fools.
When he finds that special one,
It is God's gift to him.
A woman bears the pains of life;
Her goal is motherhood.
When she finds that special one,
It is naturally understood.
Vintage Is Our Love.

Seasoned with the taste of time,
Renewed by eternity,
Vintage Is Our Love.

A woman shares the stress and strain
From problems of day-to-day.
Still, she remains so calm and cool,
Using love as her only tool.
Love, they say, is priceless—
Rare as a black pearl.
When you find that vintage girl,
You will never ever leave her.

## SOMEONE I USED TO LOVE

I remember the madness, the God-given gladness,
Of joy words were not meant to express.
I remember the tears and the difficult years
When clouds tried to darken our path.

But most of all, I can recall,
What life and I cannot forget,
That special Someone That I Used To Love,
Whom I can never forget.

How clear it still appears
Through misty memorable years,
When time was a never-ending stream
Flowing through our hearts with ease.

But most of all I can recall
What life and I cannot forget,
That special Someone That I Used To Love.
For, which I have no regrets.
Visions chase this heart of mine
With unforgettable dreams,
Clinging to space and time
Through years of fantasy.

FAITH, LOVE AND LIFE

## AFTER LOVE

I never had anyone give my love back to me.
Then you came and gave your heart, yet I turn up
empty, baby.
After love where would I be?
After Love.

Something strange comes over me,
Knowing never to taste your love again.
I try to look within my heart;
answers come within me.
Come share my fantasy and make my
dreams come true.
We will ride the clouds through eternity, and kiss,
The morning after, you and me.
If you had my heart, where would I be?
The tenderness, you give your best,
Always giving, never to receive.
I remember the laughter,
The tears, and the pain.
I close my eyes only to see your smile.
After Love, where would I be? After Love.

## WHEN I'M MISSING YOU

When I'm lonely and feeling blue,
I think about happiness
And, it comes out to you.
Though I may smile, as I gaze into your eyes,
It comes as no surprise;
For you are my sunrise.
Let me take you to a place of love and joy,
Being with you baby,
Loving you more and more.

Kissing you when I'm missing you
Makes my heart skip a beat;
For you are my dear loved one
And your kiss is such a treat.
Though I may smile, as I gaze into your eyes,
It comes as no surprise;
Someday you'll be my bride.

So wherever I go your spirit is with me.
And everybody knows
I can't find the words that would explain
All that you mean to me.
So let me take you to that place of love and joy,
Together forever, girl, that's all I'm dreaming of?

## MADNESS IN LOVE

It's been more than an hour or a day
Since I've touched you or kissed
You in love or play.
Yet somehow, the years won't keep us apart;
It's madness in love that we stay.

You are the real in my childhood fantasy,
Filling my life with joy and harmony.
These are the reasons
That I'm knocking at your door,
Wanting you forever and ever
And still more.
And yet it feels so good to be near—
As the sun guides us to each other's arms.
It's madness. Oh! It's gladness,
A power stronger than you or I!

We used to ride out on Sundays
To see the beautiful homes,
How lovely the thought that one would be our own.
A garden with a fruit tree and a swing in the back,
Higher and higher we would go and that's a fact.
It's madness. Oh! It's gladness,
A power stronger than you or I!

## BE FOR REAL

We got to be for real, be for real.
We got to be for real
Be For Real.
People everywhere do you really care?
From one place to another,
Calling on your brother,
We got to be for real, be for real.
We got to be for real, be for real.

Hollywood's in Cherry Hill—
Split homes dangling,
Forty mortgage years.
The house is jamming
But nobody is home
So be for real, my boy.

Take off your false eyelashes
And your painted lips.
Come on and get down with me
Because natural is hip.
All your naked pre teen habits
And your fantasized mind,
Will take you from
Reality in time.
I say you got to Be For Real!

FAITH, LOVE AND LIFE

## I WISH YOU WELL

We close our mouths for our hearts to speak
Of their past and present
Deciding this, for our hearts did wish
For the truth they only could tell.
But since realizing your love has gone,
How strange my life does seem;
For you taught me the meaning of love
And destroyed it by leaving my dream.
But I wish you well, because I still care
Yes, I wish you well, a love that wasn't fair.

I remember our days by the sea;
How warm and bright they seem.
The spring-like breeze and bending trees
So perfect in harmony.
But our love didn't last, and I watched it pass
Like a sailboat in the breeze.
Yes, it brought me to my knees.
Still I beckon to, with a love that was true.
You replied by saying softly bye, bye, and bye!
But I wish you well, because I still care
Yes, I wish you well, a love that was not fair.
In my arms, I'd love to hold you.
Can't you tell? I wish you well!

## IT'S DEEP LOVE

I look in your eyes and see you unsatisfied.
Yes, I can tell when things are going well.
Girl, I want to grab you, hold you, and say I care;
I'm here, and will always be when you need
Someone to share your life!
Life is moving fast; catch it while it lasts,
Can't wait another day too share your love.
Time has made me realize with you by my side,
No mountains too great to climb,
No mystery too complex to unfold.
I should have told you long ago, really.
Let you know I can hear your thoughts and feel your
pains. I will be whatever you want,
And give whenever you need!

I see your face in my dreams.
I hear your voice call to me!
I know just where you'll be, waiting so patiently!
I sometimes wake up in a cold sweat, thinking about
you. And I reach! Yes, reaching for your love,
Come a bit closer to me sugar!
You're not close enough;
I want to feel your heart beat next to mine!
Beating up and down, beating up and down!
'Cause everyone has someone to believe in,
So why not believe in me?
As every dawn has its day,
So share mine with me!
And we'll go on and on!

FAITH, LOVE AND LIFE

### IF I HAD A CHANCE

Yesterday we had a fight
Over words that were misunderstood.
I wanted to apologize
But lost the tender moment that I could.
I thought, after you had gone,
Of just how much you meant to me,
and how I'd misused your love
and sent you crying on your way.
If I had the chance to love you, just once again,
There'd be no more tears, only joys
When I'm near you.
If I had the chance to love you,
No sad songs would I sing.

Summer strides to Fall, as Spring is a day late to
December still, I remember all the promises
I once made to you—
All the grief and despair, distrust in the air.
Forgive me, little darling.
If I had the chance to love you just once again,
There'd be no more tears, only joys
When I'm near you.
If I had the chance to love you,
No sad songs would I sing.
Never would I disrupt your gentle life, little darling!
Loneliness has no friends, our love never to end.
Feel it in your heart, you and me are one part.
Going to keep on trying. If I had a chance.

## OUR LOVE IS THROUGH

We started out with a love so rare
No one knew the words quite to compare.
How perfect it all seemed, our hopes and our dreams.
Nothing could ever tear us apart; we loved each other
Deep within our hearts. But out of lust, distrust
somehow filled the air.
We both realized love was no longer there.

You'd cry only to deny of another. Did you care?
With each tear, love faded to no more.
It hurt me more than you will ever know,
The pain the hurt, will it ever go?
Let the world only hear the smiles we once knew—
Not knowing our love is really, really through.

## DISTANCE LOVE

I love you from afar;
I reach to you.
Do we believe
Half of what we see,
None of what we hear?
Do you see me
As I see you
Through the glazed eyes that fall short
Of a newborn pioneer
Focused on light?

Can you hear that beat which resounds
Deep within the channel
Walls of a maze called heart?
It resonates
The essence of your being.
Clearly, do you hear me?
Or in you're magnificence,
Does the beauty within these walls
Echo for love,
All love, any love, or my love?

## WHAT WOULD IT MEAN?

If I kissed you
And made love to you,
Told you that I loved you
And wanted you by my side,
Would it mean that I love you?
Or flirted for that selfish moment?

If I touched you
Where I've never touched you before
And might never touch you again,
Would it mean?
That I didn't enjoy you?
If I move in a way
That stayed on your mind day after day,
Would that mean
That you enjoyed my love?
And if I'm not around
Close enough to hear
The sound of your voice,
Would you smile upon my memory?

If you speak to me
Within the walls of your sanity,
Would that make you crazy?
Crazy for me?
If I laid next to your body
And never touched you,
But spoke words to make you shiver,
Did I make love to you?

FAITH, LOVE AND LIFE

## *LIFE* —

*The elements that comprise this world—
the known, and unknown — its mysterious
values that we call existence.*

## THE CHALLENGE

Courageously I was born into a world.
Lost to humanities,
Impatiently I struggle, because I got to find me.
Though I was asked so many times
Just what I'd like to be,
Only to reply I've got to find me.
It's a challenge, a game I'd like to win.
It's a challenge; first prize is to find an end.

I knew it wouldn't be easy
To find my place in time;
For hatred and jealousy will try to blow my mind.
But strange as it may seem,
There's a place for you and me—
Hand-carved with love
And sent from above-your destiny.
It's a challenge—
The kind I'd like to win.
It's a challenge—
Give me the strength and the will.
Everybody clap your hands for what you feel inside.
Everybody clap your hands for what you realize.
It's the challenge.

## WHY WORRY

I can't worry about what I can't control.
Few things are for certain—
Other than death—
And even more are true.

See a picture painted on a wall
Visions seem true yet they are different,
From me to you.
Hear simple melodic words that remind us
Of people, places, and things.
Don't let a moment pass without
Saying what it means to you.
This moment may never ever come again,
To express what it means to you.

## MOM AND DAD

Mom and Dad thank you for the times.
Grateful I am, for your heart is mine.
I've loved the life that I've shared with you.
Now life is calling. O' can't you see!
Mom and Dad, someday you will be proud of me,
For I am a reflection of you,
And will surely bring happiness too.
So I'll go on, and I'll stand tall,
The time is now, right now.

Every child got to pave their way
In a world like today!
The morning rays bring such a guiding light,
And every child is going to be all right.
Mom and Dad, how you've taught me well,
To always believe in GOD,
And lay my head in prayer.
Life is calling, calling for me.
The time is now, right now.

## I'D RATHER BE BURIED DEAD! THAN ALIVE!

Give me a job in a nightmare
Where no one really cares,
Maniacs as my henchmen, keeping
Bullies safe and sound!
Give me goals that can't be met
To keep me nosing around.
Maybe I'm good or maybe I'm bad.
But here's the way it sounds.
I'd Rather Be Buried Dead Than Alive!

Zombies walk and talk in a trance
Doomed to boredom time,
Hoping the stars will shine on them
To ease their troubled minds.
They'd like to be free of poverty,
For home is upward bound.
Maybe it's right or maybe it's wrong
But here's the way it sounds.
I'd Rather be Buried Dead Than Alive!

Isolation has them mistaken,
Buried deep in debt.
Noise from those old creepy places
Rumbles with their breath.
They'd like to be free of poverty,
For home is upward bound
I'd Rather be Buried Dead Than Alive!

### FEEL THE NEED TO BE

I was told that life was a shadow
That passes and fades.
We are living in God's hands
From day to day.
Life is but a dream
That will forever be in my heart.
There will be no others
Who will play my part.

Bid it welcome while the others
Say good-bye.
'Cause life itself is eternal
And will never die.
I will know of love and hate
And feel the need to be.
Don't ask of life
But try a bit of life.
Feel the need to be, feel the need to be.
Feel the need, feel the need to be.

## LESSONS LEARNED

I've chased the rain
Through the flames of desire
And conquered the spirit of disappointment.
I've seen through the eyes of the hope
syndrome, and kept my pride with my sanity.
But how about you?
While you've been chasing a dream,
Can you still see through the clouds of reality?
Are you dealing with the drought that finds you
When you're down and out?
Has your love kissed you a tearful good-bye?
Are you in need of a shoulder to lean upon?
Hold your head high;
Don't quit.
And pray that tomorrow comes
Wishing you the best
As you travel with faith.
Just chalk it up as
Lessons Learned.
And enjoy this dream journey.

## GET THE MONKEY OFF MY SHOULDER

I got to get this monkey off my shoulder;
so that I can breathe.
Got to get this monkey off my shoulder;
It's time for me to leave.
So you've been living your life.
Still you're not satisfied.
But can you take it, take it in stride?
Inner frustrations can surely get you down.
Relief of aggravation is nowhere to be found.
I got to get this monkey off my shoulder;
so that I can breathe.
Got to get this monkey off my shoulder;
it's time for me to leave.

Round, and around, and around I go.
Wherever I stop, the monkey knows.
Why don't you catch a ship and sail beyond the skies,
Through space and time and tell the story why?
So much confusion, distrust in the air.
Is there anybody, anywhere, who really, really cares?

## ANIMAL ATTRACTIONS

There's an animal attraction when
I look into your eyes.
Can't put my finger on it, baby,
But it's driving me wild.
I want to do all the things that animals do,
But much, much more
I want to do it with you.
Like Dr. Jackal and Mr. Hyde,
I'm not all that you see.
Come share my kingdom with me, baby.
I will make you my queen,
But most of all we will have a ball
Like the animals do,
And come together in stormy weather and do what's
natural to do.
Animal attraction, when I look into your eyes
Animal attraction, and it's driving me wild.

## DANCE TOWN U.S.A.

If you want to party
Or have a lot of fun
I'll tell you where to go
To get the job done—
At the Dance Town, Dance Town; Dance Town USA.
This is where it's happening
All of the time.
We're making heavy rhythm
Enough to blow the mind
At the Dance Town, Dance Town; Dance Town USA.

In this city
There's no sitting down,
No stooping or standing,
Everybody's getting down
At the Dance Town, Dance Town; Dance Town USA.
We got good vibrations
Going across the land,
Enough to shake a nation
From sea to sand
At the Dance Town, Dance Town; Dance Town USA.

## DREAM YOUR DREAM

Dream your dream, as all living things,
Until morning calls for you, my child.
Never look back nor regret,
what might have been.
Understand the present and what shall be
So helpless and small,
I recall you not long ago—
A bee buzzing in your own way to be free,
So much sincerity in your eyes I see.
And one day I hope to be part of your destiny.
So dream your dream, because you are a child.

Wide-eyed to this world,
Full of fire and light of this day and tomorrow.
Grow wings, my child, and catch your star.
Fly high and far.
Sail beyond this sky and space.
Touch all and learn to sing harmony
With every living thing.
But most of all, when the wind whips against all
odds, and lights are dim
or seem so hard to find,
Dream your dream.

## ANYTHING YOU WANT TO DO

Anything, anything, anything, you want to do.
If you want to ride a bike
In the middle of the night
Or saddle up a horse, of course,
It is all right with me.
Anything you want to do, baby,
It is all right with me.
As long as we are doing it together,
Whatever, forever.
Anything, anything, anything, you want to do.

If you want to freak out
'Cause that's what it's all about,
To make love beneath the stars above, baby,
Anything you want to do, baby,
It's all right with me.
As long as we are doing it together,
Whatever, forever.
Anything, anything, anything, you want to do.

## RISE

Rise and move from side to side.
You will find a big surprise
If you would simply rise.
Let your body be free
For what is natural to be—
A dancing partner with me.
Don't you hesitate.
'Cause it is never too late
To move your body endlessly.

Rise and move from side to side.
You'll find a big surprise
If you would simply rise.
Don't you hesitate.
'Cause it is never too late
To move your body endlessly.

Your personality will set you free,
From any fears you have inside.
Rise and dance with me.
Rise and let your mind be free.

## CITY MADE OF FIRE

City made of fire
Standing straight and tall,
Hear the angels calling
Before your castle falls.
Receive the awakening,
that's yours and mine alone.
Summon all the children;
Bless the ones who roam.
Daily day of mischief
Shakes the morning dew;
Be ready for the coming
The change of old to new

City made of fire
Eyes are watching you.
Prepare young hearts tomorrow;
It's time to build anew.

### COME TO ME

This world goes through so many
different changes, more than enough to,
drive anybody crazy.
But when the burdens of life,
get too heavy for your shoulders.
Come to me.
So you found that your old man
was not what you thought him to be.
He spoke smooth and easy,
but his life was kind of shady.
Don't run from hurt to hurt
trying to ease your sorrow.
Come to me.

You've got all the charm
any one man could appreciate;
yet you doubt yourself constantly.
Personality is your beauty, simply
when you're being you.
Believe me, lovely lady; yes,
I know your gentle hello.
Come to me.
I won't be able to heal the hurt,
but somehow, with love,
I'll ease the pain.
I won't be able to change the wrong,
But give you strength to carry on.
Come to me.

## IS IT TRUE?

Last night as I was out on the town,
I saw a very strange thing
Going down—
People of all shapes, sizes and forms
Confused with themselves, and hypnotized.
Are you really doing the things that you should do?
And is your heart living with your mind,
Is it true?

I know that life is really a disco drag
With fads coming in, and out so fast,
But don't you be left on your pedestal.
Just meet your maker and you shall see.

## THE LONELIEST MAN

Seems my love has gone and left me.
She has gone for another;
Now I don't know where to turn.
I'm hurt and feeling all alone,
I can't imagine anyone
being as lonely as I am now.
No one could imagine
having these tears in their eyes.
They are the tears of loneliness,

And I'm crying because I hurt for your love.
I'm the loneliest man in the world
And I'm crying because I hurt for your love.
I'm the loneliest man in the world

Could it be that my love will be
Sent straight from the Heavens above,
And I'm not to worry
'Cause love is going to come?
Love's going to come.

## IT'S NOT OVER UNTIL IT'S OVER

You thought that time had
Got the best of me?
And that our love would
Never ever be?
Surly you knew my heart
Could never be at peace,
Until your love,
Completed my fantasy.

I've been down and out
So many times before
Without a love like yours
To set my spirit free.
But, by the count of three
I guarantee, you will be mine.
Time is on our side.
Love will never die.
It's not over till it's over.
So never count me out, baby.
It's not over till it's over.
So believe in me.

One thing's for sure I'm crazy,
So crazy about you.
And it's true that I'd do anything for you.

## REACH OUT AMERICA

Reach Out America with AT&T;
They've got opportunity calling
With conveniences sure to please.
Purchase time by the hour,
Will come together to fit your needs,
Reaching out to America with a plan
That truly guarantees!
Try their free and easy to use charge cards.
It's speedy with convenience too.
Most of all, it's economical, assuring the best for you.
Reach Out America with AT&T,
With the plan, the pride, the red, white and blue.
AT&T, they've been doing it
For over one hundred years.
They're renewing it, assuring the best for you.
They keep doing it, they're renewing it.
Reach Out America with AT&T,
They've been doing it for over one hundred years.

***NINE ELEVEN—***

Angels are singing from heaven—
Remember me on Nine Eleven.

## A BIRD'S POINT OF VIEW

Look at man—
Straight, tall, short, fat, skinny.
He is all that; but he could never be me.
I am bird.
I fly from tree to tree,
Man could never be me.
I have wings,
I live constantly on the edge,
of bending limbs.
He can only hope to be what I am.
My shelter is mother earth,
My food is stored in the bosom of her breast.
I shop daily and hoard nothing more
Than I can consume,
and give life to others.
I sing every morning,
To give thanks for each day.
My melodies can never be transposed,
I captivate you with my soul.
You can only try to be like me,
I am Bird.

## I AM A POET

I am a poet in motion,
I live it; breathe it.
I was born to reason with the winds of time-—
Engage you with thoughts that are mine.
I'm a verse in a book,
In the chapter of life, that comprises man.
I dance with words, like Fred Astaire.
Dazzle you like the fresh smell of spring air,
I'm old school renewed.
I play by honor decency God's rule—
I love grass, trees, a cool breeze.
I enjoy the simple things
Like fine foods an occasional glass of wine.
I am a Poet, given of thoughts to words,
A storyteller forever.
I am old school rhythm and blues.

## BONES AND BISCUITS

Smells nice, brown with glazed dots—
Shaped like a bone, thought it would be tasty.
Never imagine this could happen.
No, not to the kid. I wonder who's watching.
The old lady searching around cat food,
Or that short gray-haired man who just
dropped the bird feed.
You think she might know who cares.
The price is right,
and I've heard it's a great treat.
It's checkout time, slow and deliberate.
I don't want to draw attention.
I wonder if the clerk,
leaning over the counter will know.
Here comes the store manager,
white short sleeved-shirt, tie, and dark
trouser. He's probably trained to recognize.
Does he care? Relax—
My palms are sweating.
Did I use deodorant this morning?
That transaction was smooth.
No one noticed a thing.
Home, sweet home and it's mealtime.
Let's try it-not bad, a bit crunchy.
Maybe I'll try it with milk the next time.
I've got to hide the box.
I have an image to up-hold.
My girl knows I don't have pets.
Now, it's Bones and Biscuits.

## TONIGHT WE ARE GOING TO PARTY

A week ago Wednesday night—
I fell down a flight of stairs.
Then my sister called me on the phone,
said my father heart had failed.
My youngest son kept us up
for two nights as well.
Seems he really had it bad
But no words could he tell.
So tonight, yes tonight—
We are going to party.

Woke up early Monday morning
the usual right on time—
Turn on the radio and it nearly blew my mind.
Heard say that I had no job,
Come join the picket line.
It would have been fine with me—
but my rent was months behind.
So tonight, yes tonight—
We are going to party.
Try to forget all our troubles, and party hardy.

## WILSON'S

She poured hot coffee,
And steam rose like a mountain cloud
beneath the morning dew.
Some folks came dressed in Sunday's best.
Others wore dreads, braids, dark shades,
high heels, spit-shine shoes and
natural hair dos.
From the kitchen, the smell of bacon beckons,
the taste buds of an old man who sat on a stool,
his lips locked, but never moving as the
waitress passed him by with Hotcakes, stacked
to the sky for all eyes to see.
"Good morning," she said, as we entered our
booth, wide-eyed, with healthy thighs
From good living and good loving.
As she winked, sirens screamed
by the window where we sat,
as if urging her on to say more.
"O, that's just the hospital across the way",
she replied to a young guest never seen before.
Side conversations ruled the air,
With indistinct dialect to burning ears,
Like toast left in a toaster too long.
These sounds engaged us all.
The biscuits are my best,
And you can get grits with your eggs.
Come sit beside me, it's friendly.
This is Wilson's on the corner of
Georgia and Avenues V;
In Washington D.C.!

## GHETTO CHILD

The laughter of your existence
wakes me at first light.
I provided you security as
You slept throughout the night.
Frail is your body because of
milk consumed by another child.
I watch you play with toys
As though a wrecking ball
bent on destruction from generations
Of your misguided greatness.
I attempt to clear your thoughts
Of the potential I see in you.
You are a Ghetto Child—
Born to fail, some say freed in an environment
That was designed for your destruction.
Your classification escapes the shelter
with delusions of your true destination.
You have allowed me to embrace
the brief fragile fragrance of hope.
"O" my Ghetto Child!

## SO FAR FROM HERE

Don't you hear me, hear me calling?
So far from here.
The stutter of my lips
Dried by the sun—
So far from here.
My hair dries from the sands
Drenched in blood of the past—
So far from here.
So far but yet near,
Close to the beat.
That beat of your heart
So heavy with guilt,
Yet light as a bedtime feather.
So far from here.
When times were good for you
Yet bad for me
Don't you hear me,
Hear me talking to you.
At night when you count sheep?
You're gold on the church table
Where you are feed seeking forgiveness.
Don't you hear me?
So far from here.
Yet, so very near.

## TEACHER'S SIGHT

He sat quietly perched in teacher's chair
each morning Immortalized in thought.
Dark wool suit, white shirt, tie, black shoes
shined. Occasionally he would canvass the
room in search of distinguished faces, as
though he could recognize more than
a voice, shape, or size.
With lesson book in one hand and
attendance sheet in the other,
Teacher sat on first bell.
His voice would bellow out.
A mournful sigh. At second bell
"Alston," "Here", I replied, bordering on
rudeness in pitch and volume only, my voice
echoed out. Next was Branch,
"Here sir", a soft, kind, beautiful girl,
(Her voice revealed this to teacher).
Next was Carter. "Carter!" Teacher yelled,
As if a crime had been committed.
"Anyone seen Carter!"

Teacher's voice scaled the ladder
As though an opera singer trembling with
disappointment.
His face, spoke a multitude of words
of lesson's learned in life that he Carter,
would discover on uncharted, grounds,

FAITH, LOVE AND LIFE

Once again Teacher yelled, "Carter! Carter!"
With pain in voice, Teacher was from the old
school. His first name was education.
Last name more education.
After third bell, you were not allowed in class.
Without a late pass.
"Ms. Branch, please deliver the attendance
sheet to the office."
Teacher's head bobbled up and down,
side to side. Silence gripped the air
With anticipation, and no Carter.
Teacher stepped to the board.
Who will take the first one?
Answered quick and correct.
You might catch an occasional smile,
rare from teacher's brow
Teacher stayed professional until the last bell.
He could not afford to let down his guard.
An unwanted voice might crowd teacher's ear.
A caring heart might ask
"Why teacher," with numbed fingers,
Legs crippled from this journey of giving.
Then, at once this crèche from broken chalk
Studded the room to a mournful roar—
Broken chalk spiraled slowly to the ground
as time, and motion engaged eyes to see.
Teacher crawling and reaching about the floor
in search of lost chalk already rolled two rows
deep beneath dirty tennis shoes,
gum rappers, and comic book favorites.
From weary arms of the prize fight un-
televised, unrecognized or seen on the main
screen,

This golden soldier of truth
With head bowed, returned to his feet and
continued his lesson. Washing windows on a
board, blurred by time. Laden with the
essence of past, present and future.
A dedicated voice spoke in the darkness.
He shared what light he had left.
For the sun never seemed to bother teacher.
I bow my head, my heart, and remember you.
My teacher, of pure unselfish thought.

## THE STREET

The street is a place to walk
To leave vulgar thoughts,
Spits on me, writes on me
And leaves its mark
I gather bodies from cities
and stack them like books.
But don't pis on me or anger me.
I don't belong to you.
You are but a visitor
Here for a short time;
I will be here for years.
Long after you have come and gone.

The old and young
All know my name
I've seen your kind before in dark places.
You are of many
Painted with the will of submission.
I await your doom and shelter your
destruction.
Walk gently, for the path is narrow
with many curves; ill will lines
my heart for you.  Blood runs my curb of
justice.  Don't doubt me.

## FADE, SKIN, LAST BLADE

Half-filled room that's good for me.
Maybe my man can cut with free hands today.
How many you got, last one, and you are next.
I can roll with that, brother.
He slowly glided to his seat.
Skin or fade one of the other barber's yelled
To his customer, dressed up in a sport shirt
and some place to go.
Give me a fade, leave a little more on the top
this time. Starting to get cool outside.
Need something to block the wind?
How are your boys doing since Patrick been
gone? They lost their identity.
Kind of like going from a bush to skin head.
No one knows who you are
Or where you're coming from.
My game is baseball.
I like the homerun and the strike out on a 3/2
pitch. Not me, yells the guy two chairs over.
B-Ball is my game-high flying,
Last minute, 30 seconds, ten, nine,
five on the shoot clock.
That's what it's all about.
A muscular heavy brother two chairs over
getting a fade yells how about the women?
That's another subject, for another time!

## CONDITIONED

I have often wondered why we do the things we do. And I have determined that it is based upon our conditioning, morals, beliefs, and how we were raised.
As a child you learn not to run because you could fall and skin your knee.
Or be stung by a bee.
Reality states that you must run, fall, and skin your knee to feel the pain.
For the next time you run, you won't fall, rather fly high.
Everyone does not have skinned knees; some have bruised minds. Which would you prefer? Anything required for the performance is conditioning.

In school you learn the golden rule, tools of your trade. To always tell the truth, and be honest as old Abe. Whose rules? Certainly not the Fifth Amendment? A prerequisite to an agreed upon condition, once you complete your educational conditioning, (I mean training) you apply for a job with an established company. Only, after it has been determined that you possess the required state of conditioning, and are prepared to train for a certain activity based upon a condition of living, you give away one-third of your life.

# FAITH, LOVE AND LIFE

You are successful at your job depending on,
the circumstances the economy and conditions
of living in our society, which will determine
your continued success. Success is not
absolute! But death and taxes are.

Like our music and movies it's very hard to
change and bring creativity with new
ideals to the forefront.
Something that is an expressed condition of
control must be done over and over again for
continued success of its conditioning
existence-maybe tweaked here and there.
Once the formula has been discovered, it
becomes something that is accustomed,
maybe a process—
Such as good morning or good night, black
Sunday, or dark day. I suspect that the
revolution and elevation of our society for
social change will first occur in our minds.
Until that time, we will exist based upon
someone else's circumstances, out of our
control. Such as the stock market as we labor
and toil raise the price of black gold. Lay five
thousands off to subsidize the cost.
Once again, we are where we were forty times
forty years ago. Attempting to free our minds
and pray that our rear ends will follow.

## EVELYN'S ASLEEP

She lays there with little motion.
When I look at her, I recall her laughter.
I am hesitant to approach her as my mother
urges me on. Speak to her;
let her know you are here.
I would like to think that my voice would be
enough—
Like a fairytale, enough to wake Evelyn.
I say to her in a soft cheerful voice
Hello, Evelyn, this is Stan, remember me?

A long tube is engaged in Evelyn's throat
to help her breathe, once only beauty gripped
her voice, to the delight of many
in the praise of God.
I'm here with my mother, sister Valeria,
and my wife Sheila.
I pause for a reaction, any reaction,
that she is alive, and can hear everything I'm
saying. I know that you're getting better; you
need your rest.
A tear enters Evelyn's eyes; she blinks. I see
your eyes blink Evelyn; does this mean you
can hear me? She blinks again, so I'm
convinced Evelyn can hear me.
I look to my mother who acknowledges
she can also see the tears and movement in
Evelyn's eyes.

Evelyn was driving on a rainy road Easter
Sunday going from one church service to
another, when her car went out of control.
Some might ask, why God, why?
I said to Evelyn, you are going to be ok!
You were put here for God to strengthen you.
This was the only way God could get your
total attention, and bring so many
people back together in his name.
Your sleep is only for a while.
Soon you will awaken!

FAITH, LOVE AND LIFE

## DUCK THE AXE

I've heard about this invisible axe;
It swings in mid air.
Some say no one controls this axe.
Yet heads fall like bowling balls,
every now and then.
With no numbers to remember
That might help you Duck the Axe,
Some say it doesn't discriminate.
Nor does it make mistakes, only eliminates.
Rather, it is a matter of balance—
Faith and sinking sand—
As we attempt to Duck the Axe.

## YES, I BELIEVE

Angels rest in a place of love—
Waiting for a silent cry
To summons them to come home
alone with all the children.
Meadows grow beneath their feet,
a guiding light for all to see.
Desert lands, giant snowflakes
to quench our hearts of sorrow.
I have this dream. Yes, I believe.
One day this world will live
in perfect harmony.
It starts with you and ends with me.
This I believe.

Above horizons stars we ride,
across the Milky Way of Life,
this wishing well for a better day
as shepherds guide our hearts to peace.
I have this dream. This I believe.
We embrace creation with a cry
only an Angel can hear.

Now I realize our Spirits are glitters of light
that eclipse the universe—
So small, yet huge with the warmth
they bring to salvation.
I saw you rise
above the carousel of birth
Into the bosom of an eternal being,
and yes, I believe.

No more hunger, no more pain,
no war, no suffering.
Birds join to sing praise.
Yes, it will be because
He told me, it will be;
I have this dream.  Yes I believe.

*A Special Thanks*

*I would like to thank the Alliance of
Telecommunication Workers of America for believing
in me.*

*I would also like to thank my neighbors,
close friends, and my family for their
Faith, Love and Life.*

■■■■■■■■■■■■■■■■■■■■■■■■■■■■■■■■■■■■■■ ı

*A Special Tribute to:*

*My father, Clarence T. Alston, Sr., my
brother, Clarence T. Alston, Jr., and Aunties for their
eternal love.*